Migrant Psalms

SERIES EDITORS

Chris Abani

John Alba Cutler

Reginald Gibbons

Susannah Young-ah Gottlieb

Ed Roberson

Natasha Trethewey

Migrant Psalms

Poems

Darrel Alejandro Holnes

NORTHWESTERN UNIVERSITY PRESS

EVANSTON, ILLINOIS

Northwestern University Press
www.nupress.northwestern.edu

Northwestern University Poetry and Poetics Colloquium
www.poetry.northwestern.edu

Printed in the United States of America

10 9 8 7 6 5 4 3 2 1

Cataloging-in-Publication Data
Names: Holnes, Darrel Alejandro, author.
Title: Migrant psalms : poems / Darrel Alejandro Holnes.
Other titles: Drinking gourd chapbook poetry prize.
Description: Evanston, Illinois : Northwestern University Press, 2021. | Series: Drinking
Gourd Chapbook poetry prize
Identifiers: LCCN 2020052886 | ISBN 9780810143586 (paperback)
Subjects: LCSH: Immigrants—United States—Poetry.
Classification: LCC PS3608.O49435645 M54 2021 | DDC 811/.6—dc23
LC record available at https://lccn.loc.gov/2020052886

for the Surge

Prayer indeed is good, but while calling on the gods a man should himself lend a hand.

—HIPPOCRATES

Contents

Foreword

Ed Roberson

In the words of its author, this chapbook "prays for a way to make sense of immigration to the United States." Though he was born in Houston, Darrel Alejandro Holnes was raised in a suburb of Panama City, Panama, to Panamanian parents, only returning to the United States at age seventeen to attend college in New Orleans. Displaced by Hurricane Katrina, he continued his education back in Houston, then attended graduate school at the University of Michigan in Ann Arbor. He lives in New York City and has lived in several cities around the Americas and Europe, including Mexico City and Berlin. Holnes knows migration.

Under the influence of his grandmother, Zilla May, a woman of faith who herself migrated from Costa Rica to Panama in the early twentieth century, and his mother, a devout Catholic, Holnes absorbed both faith and spirituality. The collection begins with "Kyrie," a long prayer form that laments and asks for mercy and clarification. Holnes describes this section as "a coming-to-America chronicle set across three years in Texas." Three staggered lines on the page in this poem display the immigrant's compromised decision of coming into what is American:

> I promise I'll be a good boy
> > a good old boy
> > > good ol' boy, yes, that's the one.
> Pray for me, TV Jesus
> or Britney Spears.

In another poem, "OTM" is a blanket acronym used by ICE to designate Spanish-speaking persons as "other than Mexican" immigrants. Holnes's poem playfully explains the distinctiveness of Panamanian within the Spanish macaronic languages of creole, pidgin, Spanglish. In Spanish, *ta bueno* translates literally as "it's good," but in Mexico it means "it's all good," whereas in Panama the same words are understood to mean "I'm official," as in "My papers are good, my money is good, I'm 'offi' or 'officially good.'"

Other complexities of the experience are shown in the distinct *amiguin*, a Mexican Spanish term for "my little friend," which the poem contrasts to the Panamanian *fren*, a take on the English word "friend," revealing the different influences of English and French on the Panamanian Spanish he grew up speaking. Holnes's poetry also gives the reader some brutal specifics of the migration through the terms coined in the process: *La Bestia* (the beast) is the train that carries people north through Central America, notorious for its lawless robbery, rape, and murder, while the *coyote* at the Mexico–US terminus of the journey is the person who helps you cross the border on foot, equally notorious as a beast for the same reasons. This poem transcends the list poem so far as to create its own unique form.

This is the form of all of Darrel Alejandro Holnes's work. The conclusion of his poem "Poder" describes and defines this original form:

> moving us farther and farther
> away from the world being just rhetoric,
> into the structure of its design
> . . .
> knowing this too is poetry.

Reader, this *is* poetry.

Acknowledgments

Some of the poems in this manuscript previously appeared in *American Poetry Review*, *Assaracus*, *Brooklyn Poets*, *Common Knowledge*, *Foglifter*, *HEArt Journal Online* (Human Equity through Art), and elsewhere in anthologies in print and online.

Migrant Psalms

Kyrie

I

It's 2005 and the pope is dead.

You don't care but I do because I'm Catholic.

Bush has just been re-elected.

I am new to Texas and America.

Houston is in the Bible Belt

    my father used to beat me with when I was bad.

I am scared   to pull Christ through my belt loops,

    he never kept my pants up back home.

It's 2005 and maybe I'll wear a skirt in Texas.

No, Texas is wearing a skirt

    & I've got mirrors on my shoes.

Do not tell her. Please?

I know you have no reason to trust me but

    St. Peter's Basilica is a megachurch

    so really, I'm just like you.

It's 2005 and this country is heaven

    so why be a good boy anymore?

Gratuitous porn is online America;

women as girls are spanked in videos referencing 1999:

    Hit me baby, one more time!

Pastor's pants sit on his ankles.

I promise I'll be a good boy

        a good old boy

                good ol' boy, yes, that's the one.

Pray for me, TV Jesus

or Britney Spears.

I know I've been bad

    but I too want the right

    to be re-elected.

In 2005, white smoke announces a new pope,

    the pungent scent of burning pages

      hangs,   ashen noose in the air.

Quick, light me like a cigarette.

Someone, have mercy,

      please save me

      from touching   or lynching

      myself.

II

It's 2006 and Twitter is a thing.

I don't care but to you it's internet poetry.

North Korea has just done a nuclear test.

140 characters against our American leader is an act

    of treason.

But ours is a free world, you say,

    and look, Seoul has no internet,

    but *my* soul is made of Wi-Fi so that can't be true.

Mother sent me an email chain of Psalm 91,

    it projects from my face when I'm angry.

Twitter invited all who forwarded the email to join its social network.

I guess God answers prayers

    through phishing scams

    or some other 21st century mysteries.

Although perhaps the Twitter thing was predictable,

the Bible has so many birds:

> @TheGreatBookofGenesis
> *God hovers over us like a dove. #BigBird #BigBrother*

> @TheBadAssBookofRevelation
> *Birds gorge on the defeated. #VultureChrist4President*

It's 2006 and my second year in Texas.

Rihanna sings "SOS" on white people radio.

It reminds my mother of "Tainted Love" by Soft Cell

when she comes to visit me from 1984.

S-O-S, please, someone help me!

Like RiRi, I too am dying for someone to help me

love this country or myself

without being labeled an online terrorist.

It's 2006 and free speech is a nuclear bomb

    since the Patriot Act

    unless you're North Korea, you say,

    where a nuclear bomb is a nuclear bomb.

But I say, perhaps nukes are just what happens

    when in 2006 you don't have the internet

    or Rihanna:

        You find a way to take over the world

            instead of just tweeting about it

            or begging for

    someone else to save you   as you join the sing-along.

III

It's 2007 and Anna Nicole Smith is dying,

    you know who she is.

    Yes, that one with the boobs.

The iPhone is new and so are my best friend's breast implants.

Her name is Chloe.

She is too short to be a model and hates her face in pictures

    though I think she's beautiful   enough

    to be my friend.

So we dye her hair blonde.

So she spends her graduation money

    on looking like Marilyn, Pamela, Madonna, Anna.

So we take selfies

    of her new breasts with my new iPhone

    and wait for Perez Hilton to tell us Anna is dead from an overdose.

We've been in a hospital waiting room before

> waiting for doctors to give us similar news when Rebecca passed away

> so it's all a little familiar.

So we don't do coke anymore.

So what? It's only MDMA.

Though it's 2007 so some people start calling it Molly.

It's my third year in Texas and I'm still finding

> so many women

> to look up to.

I'm happy to be a man;

> my wanting badly to be Molly is the closest I've come

> to wanting a sex-change, you could say

> if you want to be provocative.

>> I'm talking about my wanting to get inside an American

>> like drugs do, so deep I can't be

>> deported.

It's 2007 and I'll never love again

      like I once did inside Chloe,

      one hand on her new tits

      the other snapping dirty pics of us

            like it's *National Geographic* in the '70s

                and we're both women of color in Vietnam

                    and the cameraman.

It's 2007 and Perez Hilton

      says we've gone too soon

      and turned into

      Lucy in the sky apple pie, floating somewhere in heaven.

Obesity is killing Americans.

But you don't care because it's 2007 and fat is the new Black

      so you take a bite

and worship us   into eternal life.

IV

It's 2008 and unemployment is rising.

You don't care but my girlfriend is pregnant

    and I'm a poet

    who's never been to war

    against poverty.

2008 is my last year in Texas; this year, it seems,

everything I touch turns to gold,

    except the child my girlfriend loses

        like you lose a needle

        when you're trying to kick the habit

        and stay middle class.

After backpacking through Europe

    my baby is somewhere in an American haystack.

I wonder if the cattle know what they're grazing.

It's 2008 and we both want to find a miracle in her bleeding love

as Leona Lewis plays on the radio

singing out as if she too had just

bled out a baby.

We make love for the last time to Leona's hit song:

I keep bleeding, keep, keep bleeding love.

In 2008 Peter's girlfriend is pregnant too

so he gets a job at Starbucks near the Galleria,

right where my girl and I broke up.

Peter starts going to church again.

He hasn't been to St. Thomas since a drunk driver

killed his brother on prom night.

He was drunk when he knocked up his girlfriend

yet refuses to end another child's life.

Every time we hang, I buy him things for his daughter

or an expensive steak dinner

hoping it will bandage my wounds.

We meet so often that by early October

I'm covered in gauze.

By Halloween I'm broke but look so much like a mummy

I don't need to buy a costume for the party anyway.

Lord, have mercy.

This year it's scary enough for me to just go as myself.

Christ, have mercy.

And on the third day of November, help me

go back home and commit my body to la tierra.

Earth to earth.

Ashes to ashes.

Nuke bomb to buxom bombshell.

No.   Wait.

      It's 2008 so Obama is running for president.

Glory be to Barack in the highest

      and *word to the mothers* of his people on earth.

Am I not worthy?   Well, maybe he's come for all us immigrants.

Gloria in excelsis Deo.

      Perhaps we are his Easter people.

      Perhaps we are his Fighting Ten.

      Perhaps we can all be Black & brown Lazarus rising again and again.

In nomine Patris, et Filii, et Spiritus Sancti

      Amen.

Poder

The difference between poetry and rhetoric
is being ready to kill
yourself
instead of your children
wrote Audre Lorde.
I say this now to the mothers who sent
their children north,
risking their babies' lives for
a better living
than chasing paper or running
from drug dealers
on the streets. The difference
between art and design means
being ready to die
for what you desire
others to achieve
through your work,
hours of your life gone forever
making a little, shiny, fragile thing.
I write to the mothers who send
their children north
never knowing if they'll make it
but hoping that even if they don't
their creations might mean more than just
the flesh and bone with which they're made
because they moved, because they desired.
So many are quick to dismiss
desire as too general a word
or this language as too simple
to power the constant thrust
towards betterment we call *life*,
but poetry is sometimes made of such things,
words used so often we take them for granted

and forget their power is in how they unite
existence through a common tongue.
In Spanish, the word for *power*
is the same as the word for *I can*.
Poder, one simple word banging the drum rhythm
made by children's soles thumping against the earth:
Po-der, po-der, po-der; the power of doing
in each disyllabic step of metric feet
moving us farther and farther
away from the word being just rhetoric,
into the structure of its design
where we find the power to turn suicide
into sacrifice, the power to turn beasts
into man, and man into martyr or miracle.
This is what makes miracles: a desire path
stretching seventeen hundred miles
through an armed border wall,
through electric barbed-wire fences—
A surge surmounting
all odds to rise beyond the stratosphere;
knowing this too is poetry.

for the Surge: Central American refugees marching to the USA

OTM, or Other Than Mexican

Other than *que pedo*
We *que xopa*

Other than *ta bueno*
We *offi*

Other than *cosa*
We *vaina*

Other than *vato*
We *pelao*

Other than *amiguin*
We *fren*

Other than *coyote*
We ride *La Bestia*

Other than *¿Mande?*
We *¿Que cosa?*

Other than *no mames*
We *chucha*

Other than *culero*
We *hijueputa*

Other than *calmate guey*
We *tranquilo pana*

Other than *me vales madre*
We *me vales verga*

Other than *peda*
We *party*

Other than *chela*
We *pinta*

Other than *crudo*
We *focop*

Other than *el arte de engañar*
We *juega vivo*

Other than *pinta*
We *sopre*

Other than *llevarse el demonio*
We *cabrea*

Other than *huir*
We *chifear*

Other than *chava*
She *gial*

Other than *bonita*
She *pritti*

Other than *firme hina*
She *pai*

Other than *casita*
We *chanti*

Other than *pachanga*
We *rumba*

Other than *panzana*
We *preñada*

Other than *padre*
We *viejo*

Other than *nene*
We *chichi*

Other than *niños*
They *children*

Other than *fresh off the boat*
They *gringos*

Other than *hablar*
They *speak*

Other than *vivir*
They *be*

Other than *nosotros*
They *me*

Naturalization

I haven't yet come out to my fam

 and I'm dating a white man named Jack.

Everyone has a part of themselves they keep private,

 these days the secret is their issue with race

 or desire. Mamá always wanted

to be American, but she'd read in *Essence* magazine

 about how its Black women

 were the least married in the country

 because ballplayers preferred white women on their arms.

Can you hear her crying

 as I play ball with my white boyfriend?

Hand jobs are the latest

 sex act in fashion. But then again,

 love is an older kind of allegiance than citizenship.

Sometimes,

 I wear a cop uniform

 during sex and throw my lover

21

behind bars. This role play is not called

    Black Lives Matter. It's called

Love and Basketball. Jack plays

    the white college ball player

I've arrested for slipping   a roofie into   my drink

    while I was undercover at a frat party.

And now, in jail,   he begs for my   forgiveness.

    I tell him no one man can save him

from a system; mass incarceration

    is the American way. But I, at least, can apply

            some lube and help   ease the pain.

Don't believe this part;

    it's too dark to be true.

                The American Dream

is not a fantasy. It's as real as   the resurrection

    of turkey on Thanksgiving   and the healing properties of   apple p

There isn't much difference these days

    between religion and history; if you believe it so,

then that's how it happened. People believe more

    in their points of view than in facts. Maybe I shouldn't

be any different. Maybe I'll just believe

    my mother already knows her son

    is in love with   Jesus or some other

    white man.   Mmm . . . yes,

I believe we all know it,   to some degree,   a truth so universal

    others, on some level, *must*   know it too,

if only they could   make belief.   Then maybe,

    just maybe,   the rest could finally

be as free or   American   as I've just now   come to be.

Amending Wall

If "crucified" means one has died
on the cross, then what is the word
in English for dying at the crossing
between countries? What word describes
when a brown woman's dreams of being
something like a white man are killed
at the intersection between his dreamt-up borders
and his dream-come-true border patrol?
"White man" like dead men printed or
minted on money more valuable
than the pesos in her purse.
"White man" like gods on horseback come to
conquer their India after reading a
mistaken map. "White man" like the grace of
misinterpreted omens turned
into a chance for vicious attack.
"White man" like buying but outlawing
cocaine to catch the "brown man" in the crossfire of
its trade. "White man" like picket fences
in award-winning films about
the privilege of being "so over"
privilege that He yearns
for something "real."
Something there is that loves
a wall, that builds a boundary, that calls
the structure "love of country."
Something there is that kills those who trespass.
Something there is that buries
bodies at a border as foundation stones
for yet another wall. But something there is that doesn't love
fathers saying, "Good fences make good neighbors."
Something doesn't love a man carving up
a continent and its people to make a new world

in the image of old words like the name of God
instead of new words like the name of one's own desires
to divide life into here and after by crossing an ocean
as if it were the pearly gates. O Amerikkka,
if anywhere there are limits are beginnings and ends,
then Heaven has to be a nothing
loving a something loving its everything;
then life, country, and their borders
ain't nothing but a thing.

after Robert Frost

The 21st Century Poem

It's the 21st century, and my ex-boyfriend is

    using my pics on Grindr.

You don't care, but I'm still modest

    and he has exposed my flesh to the elements,

        to the trolls, to the screenshots . . .

It's the 21st century, and Atlanta has the same HIV rate as Zimbabwe,

    so I'm on PrEP to keep Grindr-ing

    Black men wearing du-rags

        into pepper

            even though I'm in New York City,

        even though I'm a Black man too

          without HIV

            and with a white boyfriend.

My mother warned me against

    the disease the first time she saw me

    thirst for a white man

    while watching Will & Grace in high school.

I was a high test-scorer back in the day.

I once tested HIV positive but

fifteen hundred vials of blood later found out

it was false. The world is full of

false positives.

"Jesus Christ! Of course it is," you say,

rolling your eyes at my chagrin.

I should know better, after all

it's the 21st century and   *Make America Great Again!*

is a sexually transmitted infection/disease.

I'm DDF, I'm negative, I'm "clean"

so when my ex leaked my dick pic online

it went viral—*semen spread everywhere!*

It's the 21st century and whenever women ask if I've had kids yet,

I always say, "None that I know of!"

"But who knows anything?"

I ask my mother. Even 23 and Me

can't really tell what race you are.

You don't care as long as your ex

thinks you're pretty enough to want back.

I think du-rags are sexy. I wish I knew

how to pull off wearing them like my

ex does in ATL.

I wish I knew how to love him

past my fear of acquiring the disease.

I wish I knew how I appeared to

people who like or steal my pics online.

Maybe out there, on the apps, is a more appealing me,

a me who is more "local" to the other dating profiles,

a me who is more "native" to this new   century

and its ways of being/seeing, being seen.

It's the 21st century and I'm still foreign—

Or is it now that I'm just too old

to compare to the picture-perfect me on Instagram?

Maybe out there, the social-media me

    has found the perfect digital mate.

Together, they are avatars   loving each other

    past programming, past algorithm, past reboot.

But maybe in flesh, I am already an avatar

    of my ancestors, a great ancient   ghost

        caught in a new skin, caught in a smart phone

            a Tupac   hologram   on tour,

            a rerun of a foreign TV show   you binge watch

    lost in an American eternity   of endless choices on Netflix.

But don't worry, you're now

    an expert navigator of such things!

Don't worry, you've become a discoverer

    with a compass and a magic ring!

Yes, that's right, reader, you're a hacker, or

    an antivirus, and somewhere

beneath the malware, disease, and hunka hunka sex appeal,

you and I have finally found—   Do you see it?   That thing

we used to call   "real."

About the Author

Darrel Alejandro Holnes is the recipient of a National Endowment for the Arts Literature Fellowship in Creative Writing (Poetry). His poems have previously appeared in the *American Poetry Review*, *Poetry* magazine, *Callaloo*, *Best American Experimental Writing*, and elsewhere. Holnes is a Cave Canem and CantoMundo fellow who has earned scholarships to the Bread Loaf Writers' Conference, Fine Arts Work Center in Provincetown, Postgraduate Writers Conference at Vermont College of Fine Arts, and residencies nationwide, including a residency at MacDowell. His poem, "Praise Song for My Mutilated World," won the C. P. Cavafy Poetry Prize from Poetry International. He is an assistant professor of English at Medgar Evers College, a senior college of the City University of New York (CUNY), where he teaches creative writing and playwriting, and a faculty member of the Gallatin School of Individualized Study at New York University.